© Copyright Little Book Publishing 2023

The world is filled with millions of people. Every day can be like living in a stadium full of people.

The crowds are cheering, the cheerleaders are shouting, and many fans are full of energy clapping and yelling. This probably wouldn't be the ideal place to read a book or study for an exam. With all the excitement going on around you, and so many things to watch, our minds begin to get in tune with all of those events happening all at once.

Our ears are fine tuned to hear many sounds and some of them we may even tune out. Of course, we can hear the sound of a jet plane flying overhead or a motorcycle rushing by, but what about the subtle sounds?

If we read a book in a small Café, chances are, we can tune out a lot of the other sounds in the room. When sitting at home during the early morning hours, with your window open, you can hear the sound of the birds chirping. These are sounds people can get around without having too much distraction. The sound of a flowing body of water can actually be a calming noise as is the sound of rain falling. So what does this all mean? Why do we need to tune out the noise? Beyond the noise is thought, deep thought.

People who have become inventors and people who are great thinkers with much wisdom and knowledge have all had to stop and focus. That is why it is so important to turn down the noise.

Isn't it amazing how often times we can daze off into space while we daydream about a specific thought? How time just seems to stop in that moment and how we seem to fade out all the background noise. Then as soon as someone calls your name, you get pulled back into the world, and you can now hear all the noise again.

There are so many studies done on how the mind works in a sleep state, but just imagine if there were more studies done on the day dreamers. I wonder what would be discovered. Maybe they would discover that day dreamers are deep thinkers and can find more solutions to problems. Maybe they would discover that day dreamers have a more creative side and can find unique ways of doing things.   All the same, the state of day dreaming is where one needs to be from time to time.   When you get on a cruise boat full of people you don't really expect to be alone or without noise, yet somehow you have managed to look out at the water and find a quiet moment. These quiet moments in life help put your life into perspective. They not only give you an insight of how to deal with situations but they can bring a moment of peace in the middle of a storm. They can give one an epiphany. Sometimes, in that simple moment it gives one a chance to just regroup themselves. When you have a lot of tension and frustration we often take a moment to cool off. This is kind of like that but with the intent of finding a little more than calming down.

I am a busy mother of 6 and know what it is like to try to keep on schedule with the things you need to get done for the day. Then one kid gets sick, the other needs a ride to practice, and the other one is hungry. I didn't learn right away how I was going to get the things I needed to get done and still fulfill everyone else's need. I made a schedule, wrote a list, and even assigned my kids chores to do, yet I still seemed to be running in circles. I still couldn't get a grasp on the day and would be completely exhausted when the day was over. It seemed like I never had time for myself and I never could focus on one thing for too long because I was trying to make time to finish something else. My only real down time was going to church. My children knew that this was my time and that they needed to behave so I could listen. Going to church became my only quiet moment of me looking out over the sea. But for the other 6 days I was going crazy. Things needed to change. I began to start to make a few minutes in the evening for myself. However, as my children entered their teenage years, their needs and desires multiplied, demanding a significant amount of my time. This left me with less opportunity to reflect and unwind, **leaving me constantly in the noise unable to clear my head.**

With all the things one must go through in life there has to come a moment of peace and reflection. I used to think watching tv was how I could relax. It is relaxing but it doesn't give you much peace. It doesn't help you to regroup and be ready to take on a new day. It doesn't help you to solve problems. TV was simply a distraction for me to not have to deal with reality. I could watch TV and not think about life until I was back on the move living and then wishing I had more time to think and reflect.

You will know when you have stopped listening to the inner you because you will be tired. You will become confused and feel like time is never on your side. I am telling you from experience, stop and listen. In a quiet place, watch how your thoughts will start coming through clearer than before. It will be like having a guide. And I will tell you this. I am not sure that I believe that there is someone out there in the spirit world just waiting to give you all the answers to life. All I am saying is that your mind is capable of growth. It can reach to limits one can only imagine. With self-awareness comes peace, and a less cluttered brain.

It took me quite a long time to really get the awareness I

was looking for because the world can take a lot of your energy. In my study to find the inner me I realized that meditation was not the only thing I needed to be aware of. With time, I realized with meditation you also must have patience. As an adult in a fast-paced moving world, having patience can be very difficult. There are so many things that we have now that people want instant gratification. There is fast food, high-speed internet, quick money, to even quick responses from your friends texting. The world says things need to be fast and always going. If you could stop time for just 1 hour, what would you do with that time? Would you still be rushing around to get things done or would you sit and relax because you have a moment that you don't need to be anywhere or do anything?

How often do you get mad and want to throw your phone when it freezes up or the internet stops working? What is the rush? The internet is always going to be there, slow or not. There will only be so many things you can get done in one day and then you have the next day. There have been times where I have waited on things that I feel should have taken a short amount of time, but they seem to last forever. Example: I ran in this retail store because I had to return an item. I know going in there that I don't have a lot of time to stop because I have an appointment, I need to get to, but this was on the way. I say to myself, "great! There is only one person in line. I should be in and out of here quickly." Of course, that wasn't the case and the store clerk had to call for help, then go back and find the item in the store and so on. I got so irritated with the situation not only because I didn't have the patience to stand there all day, but I had another appointment. See, I am one of those people that likes to get all of their work done so at the end of the day I can relax. But at the end of my days, I never finish this lengthy list of tasks. Which then means I don't get to relax. Instead, I find myself trying to figure out how to get the things I missed out today on tomorrow's task list. When we battle with patience it takes away our peace. Besides, what is the rush? Either tomorrow is promised to us or it isn't. Getting one more thing done isn't going to make much of a difference in our life. The quality of how we choose to spend the time we have in our lives is what is most important.

It is important that at the end of the day we are satisfied with the outcome of our day and our lives. That each day we are finding out more about ourselves and understanding the world. Our life journey is to grow. Not just physically but mentally.

What is the definition of Meditation?
In short, meditation is the act of focusing on deep thought or a way to self-reflection. It can be a way to find clarity and used for relaxation. Meditation can be used to reduce stress, refocus and find self-awareness.
Meditation is a practice that can help you calm your mind,

reduce stress, and improve your overall well-being.

Who uses meditation?
It is important to understand how meditation is used because when people hear this word they automatically think of chanting in a religious group, cult, or some kind of dark magic practice. Meditation is used in so many ways. Yes, religion is in fact one of them. Doctors use this method for patients that have suffered a great tragedy or loss in their lives. It is also used for anxiety.

Meditation helps refocus one's attention span, decrease blood pressure, and also can help improve one's sleep.

How does Meditation work?
Meditation gives the mind a chance to work in a different playing field. Meditation gives the brain a chance to look past what the world calls limitations and gives you a chance to see a greater possibility. It gives you a chance to see and desire change.

I am not saying meditation will bring you prosperity in wealth. What it will do is open your eyes to an awareness level beyond what you are familiar with. We have already spoken about the noise, so think about how much noise is going on in your day. Do you get a lot of time to meditate or refocus? Does your job or home situation make it hard to get a moment to yourself?

Meditation

So, how do we get ourselves into the state of quiet. This is truly easier to show someone than it is to write it. For meditation can take some practice. Meditation can be as simple as closing your eyes and focusing on one thought. Seems easy enough but what if you were in Las Vegas? Would you be able to meditate with the lights, crowds, and noise?

Now let's begin with how one can reach these levels of awareness.

Here are some steps to get started.

1. **Find a quiet and comfortable place**: Choose a space where you can sit without distractions for the duration of your meditation practice. You can sit on a cushion or chair with your back straight, or even lie down if that is more comfortable for you.

2. **Set a time limit**: Decide on how long you want to meditate for. As a beginner, start with a shorter time period, such as 5 or 10

minutes, and gradually increase the time as you become more comfortable with the practice.

3. **Focus on your breath**: Close your eyes or lower your gaze and begin to focus on your breath. Take deep breaths, inhaling through your nose and exhaling through your mouth. Focus on the sensation of your breath moving in and out of your body. If your mind wanders, gently bring your attention back to your breath.

4. **Observe your thoughts:**

As you continue to focus on your breath, you may notice thoughts popping up in your mind. Rather than trying to push them away, simply observe them and let them go. Imagine your thoughts like clouds passing by in the sky. Acknowledge them, but don't get caught up in them.

5. **End your practice**: When your time is up, slowly open your eyes and take a few deep breaths. Take a moment to notice how you feel and try to carry that sense of calm and relaxation

with you into the rest of your day.

Remember that meditation is a practice, and it takes time and patience to develop. Don't be discouraged if you find it difficult to quiet your mind at first. With practice, you will become more comfortable and start to experience the benefits of meditation.

Finding inner peace can be a journey that requires patience, practice, and self-reflection. Here are some steps you can take to work towards finding inner peace:

1. Practice mindfulness: Mindfulness is the practice of being present in the moment, without judgment or distraction. It can help you become more aware of your thoughts and emotions and develop a greater sense of inner calm. You can practice mindfulness through meditation, yoga, or simply taking a few moments to focus on your breath throughout the day.

2. Cultivate gratitude: Focusing on what you are grateful for can help shift your perspective and bring a sense of positivity and contentment to your life. You can take a moment each day to express gratitude for the people and experiences in your life.

3. Let go of negativity: Holding onto negative emotions such as anger, resentment, or regret can weigh heavily on your mind and prevent you from finding inner peace. Practice forgiveness, both towards others and yourself, and try to let go of past hurts or mistakes. This can help you release negative emotions and move forward with a greater sense of calm and acceptance.

4. Connect with nature: Spending time in nature can be a powerful way to cultivate inner peace. Whether you take a walk in a park or hike in the mountains, being surrounded by natural beauty can help you feel more grounded and connected to the world around you.

5. **Practice self-care**: Taking care of your physical, emotional, and spiritual needs can help you feel more balanced and at peace. This can include things like getting enough sleep, eating a healthy diet, exercising regularly, spending time with loved ones, and pursuing hobbies or interests that bring you joy.

Remember that finding inner peace is a journey, and it

may take time and effort to achieve. Be kind and patient with yourself and focus on making small changes that can have a big impact over time.

Drowning out noise can be challenging, but there are several strategies you can try to help reduce external distractions and create a more peaceful environment:

1. Use noise-cancelling headphones or earplugs: If you're in a noisy environment, noise-cancelling headphones or

earplugs can be an effective way to block out external sounds and help you focus on your work or relaxation.

2. Play white noise or soothing music: Listening to white noise or soothing music can help mask external noises and create a calming background sound. You can find a variety of white noise apps or playlists online or create your own playlist of calming music.
3. Create a quiet environment: If possible, try to create a quiet environment by closing

windows and doors, turning off electronics, and minimizing other sources

Through my personal experience, I have found that learning how to quiet the mind has been extremely helpful in solving various problems throughout my life. During moments when I felt hopeless in finding a solution, meditation had allowed me to access answers out of thin air, which felt almost surreal to me. I was amazed by how effortless it became to tackle complex issues once my mind was free of distractions.

I can't say that every problem was solved with meditation, but many have. Sometimes when I lay down to sleep after a busy day. Super tired that I know when my head hits the pillow that I will be right to sleep. But some nights that simply wasn't the case. As my body entered a state of rest and relaxation, I found that my mind began functioning in extraordinary ways. It's during these moments that I often receive inspiration for my next book or experience a profound sense of peace and joy. Such moments leave me feeling fulfilled and grateful for another day of life, and for the opportunity to encounter new experiences that add meaning to my existence.

As my body entered a state of rest and relaxation, my mind began to operate in extraordinary ways, exceeding my imagination. It is during these moments that I would get new book ideas. When getting these new ideas I would be excited and have a deep sense of peace. This feeling fills me with gratitude for another day of life, where each day presents opportunities to experience something new compared to the previous day.

Another area to keep an I on is criticism. People often tend to criticize others, which is surprising to think about. Unfortunately, this happens all too frequently and can lead to a lot of discouragement. While meditation can help alleviate stress and clear the mind, it is equally important to grow a positive state of mind.

When you manage to silence the noise and engage into deep thoughts, it is crucial to remember not to let external factors control your inner peace and thoughts. Despite living in the middle of chaos, it is vital to recall the serene place within you and refocus to regain that sense of peace. Discover self-gratitude in your actions and remain self-encouraged when faced with discouragement from others. Reflect on why someone speaks ill of you. Do they have an ulterior motive or are they simply projecting their own unhappiness onto you? Perhaps, they are even curious about how you consistently maintain a positive mindset, as they observe you in that state.

Learning how to ignore criticism is a valuable skill that can greatly contribute to our emotional well-being and personal growth. It involves developing a resilient mindset and a strong sense of self-worth. Here are some key points to consider:

1. Self-awareness:
Recognize that criticism is often subjective and reflects the perspectives and preconceptions of others. Understand that you have the power to determine your own self-worth.

2. Evaluate the source:
Consider the credibility and intentions of the person offering the criticism. Not all feedback is constructive or helpful. Focus on feedback from trusted and reliable sources, while disregarding

baseless or malicious comments.

3. Reinterpret criticism:
View criticism as an opportunity for growth and self-improvement. Instead of taking it personally, extract valuable insights and use them to enhance your skills or abilities.

4. Confidence in your abilities:
Develop a strong belief in your own capabilities and trust in your decisions. Recognize that you are the expert of your own life and

that external opinions should not define your worth or dictate your path.

5. Surround yourself with support:
Build a network of positive and encouraging individuals who uplift and inspire you. Seek guidance and feedback from those who genuinely want to see you succeed.

6. Practice self-care:
Engage in activities that boost your self-esteem and well-being. Take time for self-reflection, engage in hobbies, and prioritize self-

care practices that help you maintain a positive mindset.

Remember, ignoring criticism does not mean disregarding all feedback or refusing to grow. It means selectively choosing which criticisms to use and using them constructively while maintaining a strong sense of self and personal worth. By embracing this mindset, you can navigate criticism with confidence, resilience, and a focus on your own personal development.

Incorporating meditation into our lives can be a transformative practice. It offers a sanctuary of stillness and relieves the chaos of everyday life. By regularly engaging in meditation, we can improve a greater sense of self-awareness, inner calm, and mental clarity. This practice not only helps to alleviate stress and anxiety but also enhances our ability to navigate challenges with resilience and self-control.

Furthermore, meditation opens the door to a deeper connection with ourselves and the world around us, developing compassion, empathy, and a profound sense of well-being. By embracing meditation as a part of our routine, we engage on a journey of self-discovery and self-care, unlocking the immense potential within us to lead a more balanced, fulfilling, and meaningful life.

The practice of drowning out the noise to focus holds tremendous value. In a world filled with distractions and constant stimulation, finding moments of silence and stillness becomes increasingly essential. By intentionally tuning out the noise and enhancing our ability to focus, we can tap into a heightened state of productivity, creativity, and clarity. This process allows us to direct our attention towards what truly matters, enabling deeper engagement with tasks, improved problem-solving abilities, and enhanced overall performance. Additionally, by creating space for focused attention, we foster a sense of mindfulness and presence in our lives, promoting greater awareness and deeper connections with ourselves and others. Therefore, by consciously choosing to drown out the noise and grow a focused mindset, we unlock our full potential and create a path towards personal growth, achievement, and fulfillment. Take the time to drown out the noise because the world is louder than we think.

www.ingramcontent.com/pod-product-compliance
Lightning Source LLC
Chambersburg PA
CBHW021125080526
44587CB00010B/643